The CHEW

APPROVED

The Most Popular Recipes from *The Chew* Viewers

Edited by Ashley Archer

KINGSWELL

LOS ANGELES • NEW YORK

PAGE 1: **Apple Crumb Cake, recipe on page 126.**

PAGE 2: **Tasty, Trashy Taters, recipe on page 38.**

Content Coordinator: Janet Arvelo

Researcher: Giselle Snyder

Food Photographer: Andrew Scrivani

Senior Food Stylist: Jackie Rothong
Food Stylists: Ian McNulty, Alexandra Utter
Assistant Food Stylist: Kelly Jenke
Prop Stylist: Soo-Jeong Kang

Cover host photographer: Lorenzo Bevilaqua/ABC

Photographer Credits:
Lorenzo Bevilaqua: 6–7, 70–71, 78–79, 89; Jeff Neira: 11, 17, 46–47, 61, 92, 94, 96–97, 100, 118–119, 128–129; Lou Rocco: 14–15, 37, 62, 104, 124; Ida Mae Astute: 24–25, 134; Fred Lee: 43, 130; Heidi Gutman: 74, 84.

All photography unless otherwise noted © American Broadcasting Companies, Inc.

For information address Kingswell, 1101 Flower Street, Glendale, California 91201.

Editorial Director: Wendy Lefkon
Executive Editor: Laura Hopper
Designer: Gregory Wakabayashi / Welcome Enterprises, Inc., New York

ISBN 978-1-4847-7639-1
ILS: FAC-008598-16253

First edition October, 2016
10 9 8 7 6 5 4 3 2 1

SUSTAINABLE FORESTRY INITIATIVE
Certified Chain of Custody
At Least 20% Certified Forest Content
www.sfiprogram.org
SFI-00993
For Text Only

Contents

We never thought of *The Chew* as just a TV show. It was always meant to be a group of friends on TV swapping recipes with a group of friends watching TV.

We have thrived on the idea that our fans know as many delicious dishes as the hosts. We have invited hundreds of viewers to stand bowl-to-bowl with our on-air family to share their prized edible heirlooms with us.

When the show is over each day, the food friendship continues online. The result is a treasure of viewer family recipes that have been tested and loved over lifetimes.

Thechew.com rattles with excitement whenever a new home-cooked hit makes it onto our Web pages. The recipe download numbers clearly inform us about what's a hit and what's a yawn. That tells us what you want to taste and treasure and put onto your own family's dinner table.

So . . . we asked ourselves one quiet afternoon on the sunny back porch of The Chew Productions this: why not serve up the best of the homemade magic in one book and sprinkle some host-cooked favorites on the side? When we factored in the family traditions behind the meals, we realized it's been hundreds of years in the making, so who are we to argue?

We hope you'll give these a shot and tell us what you think. Feel free to join our "little" club of food-loving friends. Send us your own recipes; there is a solid chance you could wind up on-air or in our next book. At the very least, you're giving a much-loved gift from your well-fed family to ours.

Gordon Elliott, Executive Producer

CHAPTER 1
Breakfast Bonanza

Oh yeah, it's breakfast time, my favorite meal of the day. Fry it, poach it, scramble it, drench it in hot maple syrup, or put it on a roll. I don't care what you do to it; I just want to eat it! Now, I try to be good during the week, which can be hard especially when our amazing viewers bring such crave-worthy creations to *The Chew*'s table. Typically, Monday through Friday, I'm an oatmeal guy. Green juice works, too, paired alongside a protein-packed veggie frittata that helps me stay full throughout the day. But on the weekends, well that's when I go big, and then I go home and take a nap!

I get really excited about eggs Benedict, cinnamon rolls, or sticky buns. And if there's corned beef hash on a menu, forget about it! And here's a secret that my wife, Liz, and I discovered after many years in the restaurant business: if you call your first meal of the day brunch, you can have a cocktail and no one will judge you for it. After a meal like that, there's only one thing to do—slip into my sweatpants and it's back on the couch just in time for the next football, baseball, or basketball game.

Now this routine has become a weekend tradition in my house. And what I find so exciting about cooking with *The Chew* viewers is learning about the traditions that they have created with their families. Each home is different, each story unique; but what they all have in common is that they are all focused on creating memories around the table. So here in this glorious chapter dedicated to what I feel is the most important meal of the day, are our favorite viewer recipes and tips from the past five years.

You guys have shown us some really creative ways to rise and dine every day of the week, and we thank you from the bottom of our hearts and bellies.

—**Michael Symon**

Irish Soda Bread

Courtesy of Bill Herlihy

Serves: 12   Prep Time: 15 minutes   Cook Time: 1 hour

MARIO: Saint Patrick's Day is a pretty big deal around these parts because Bill Herlihy, our Executive in Charge of Production, brings in loaves and loaves of his family's famous Irish soda bread for *The Chew* crew. The recipe has been around for generations, and let me tell you, it causes quite the feeding frenzy around the office. After a lot of begging, we were finally able to get Bill to give up his secret family recipe for what we feel is the best soda bread ever created. It's light and flaky, baked to perfection, almost like a giant biscuit or scone. Served warm with a little salted Irish butter, it's ideal for any breakfast or afternoon snack.

3½ cups all-purpose flour, plus more for dusting

¼ cup sugar

1 teaspoon baking powder

1 teaspoon baking soda

¾ teaspoon salt

½ cup (1 stick) unsalted Irish butter, cut into small cubes and frozen

1 8-ounce container sour cream, at room temperature

1 large egg, at room temperature

2 cups raisins

1 cup buttermilk, at room temperature

1 teaspoon caraway seeds (optional)

Salted Irish butter, to serve

1. Preheat oven to 375 °F with a rack set in lower third part of oven.

2. Line a baking sheet with parchment.

3. In a large bowl, whisk together flour, sugar, baking powder, baking soda, and salt.

4. Add the butter to the dry ingredients, tossing to coat, and press between fingers until the mixture resembles coarse, wet sand. Then, stir in the sour cream and egg. Stir in the buttermilk, then the raisins and caraway seeds (if using) and mix until sticky dough forms.

5. Turn dough out onto a lightly floured work surface. Using a floured bench scraper, form into a round loaf. Using a sharp knife, score a large "X" in the center.

6. Place on the prepared sheet pan and transfer to oven. Bake until loaf is golden brown and a toothpick inserted into the center comes out clean, about 1 hour. If top begins to brown too quickly, loosely cover with a piece of aluminum foil.

7. Transfer to a wire rack to cool.

8. Slice and serve slathered with softened, salted Irish butter.

Eggs Purgatory

Courtesy of Antoinette Lordo

| Serves: 4 | Prep Time: 5 minutes | Cook Time: 10 minutes |

CARLA: This recipe comes from one of our favorite regulars on *The Chew*, Grandma Antoinette. She is an incredibly talented cook and a fierce competitor. She has taken home the title of Iron Grandma not once, but twice in our studio, both times crushing the competition with her delicious family recipes. This dish is a riff on the classic Italian dish "eggs in hell," but as she puts it, hers is "a little more well behaved" and a lot less spicy. Her winning recipe starts with a slice of toasted Italian bread that's topped with an egg over easy; creamy, herbed ricotta; gooey provolone cheese; and tangy marinara. It's a real winner!

1 cup ricotta cheese

1 teaspoon parsley leaves, finely chopped

Kosher salt and ground black pepper, to taste

4 tablespoons sharp provolone cheese, grated, plus more

2 tablespoons butter, plus 2 tablespoons for buttering toast

4 extra large eggs

½ cup marinara sauce (store-bought)

4 slices seeded Italian loaf, cut on bias, about ½–¾-inch thick

2 tablespoons extra-virgin olive oil

5 or 6 basil leaves, chopped to garnish

1. Preheat broiler to high.

2. In a medium bowl, stir together the ricotta, parsley, 4 tablespoons of the provolone, salt, and pepper. Set aside.

3. Heat an oven-safe medium nonstick skillet over medium heat. Add the 2 tablespoons butter and melt.

4. Crack the eggs into the pan and fry on one side. Sprinkle with salt and pepper.

5. Remove the pan from the heat and flip eggs. Top each egg evenly with the ricotta mixture and the marinara and top with the remaining provolone. Drizzle with olive oil.

6. Transfer the pan to the oven and cook just to melt the cheese. Make sure not to overcook the eggs. The yolk should still be runny.

7. Toast the sliced bread while the eggs are baking.

8. Butter the toast and top each piece with an egg. Sprinkle fresh pepper and chopped sweet basil to garnish.

TIP: Switch things up and serve a variation for lunch or dinner! Just substitute a breaded chicken cutlet or thinly sliced sautéed eggplant for the eggs and you've got yourself a delicious open-faced sandwich that's perfect for any time of the day. **—Mario**

Feta, Spinach, Sweet Potato Frittata

Courtesy of Kristine Hoskins

| Serves: 6 | Prep Time: 10 minutes | Cook Time: 20 minutes |

MICHAEL: Kristine, you had me at feta! I probably eat some form of frittata for breakfast about three times a week, and when you put a Mediterranean twist on it, oh honey, I'm in heaven. What I love about a frittata is that it really is the most delicious way to clean out your fridge. You've got leftover sausage and broccoli: frittata! Last night's fajita fillings: frittata! It's a fantastic way to reimagine your leftovers, and there are so many interesting flavors packed into Kristine's, it's no wonder she came out on top, winning the title of Baroness of Breakfast!

1 tablespoon olive oil

3 slices of pancetta, cut ¼-inch thick

1 sweet potato, peeled and cut into ½-inch dice

¼ Vidalia onion, peeled and diced

1 rosemary sprig, leaves only, chopped

6 cups spinach

8 eggs

¼ cup half-and-half

Kosher salt and ground black pepper, to taste

⅛ teaspoon nutmeg

¼ cup feta cheese, crumbled, plus more to garnish

1. Preheat oven to 425 °F.

2. Place a nonstick skillet over medium high heat. Add the pancetta with a tablespoon of olive oil and cook until fat renders, about 4 minutes.

3. Add the sweet potato, onion, rosemary, and a sprinkle of salt and pepper. Cook until potato softens, about 8 minutes. Add the spinach and cover until wilted.

4. Remove half of the spinach-potato mixture from the pan and set aside.

5. Beat eggs with half-and-half and a pinch of salt and nutmeg. Add the eggs to the pan, mix with a spatula, and then add the reserved potatoes and spinach to the top of the semi-scrambled eggs.

6. Top with the feta. Bake until eggs are firm, about 5–8 minutes. Sprinkle with additional Feta and cut into wedges to serve.

VIEWER TIP: *The Chew* viewer Jenn from Delaware has a great tip for keeping bugs and dust or sand out of your drink when throwing an outdoor brunch! Just take a cupcake liner and cut a tiny hole in the center at the base. Then push a straw through the hole. Turn the liner upside down and place it over the top of your glass as a lid for your drink. You can also customize the liners by writing your guests names right on top so that you have no trouble keeping up with your cocktail. **—Clinton**

Monday Morning Breakfast Burrito

Courtesy of Lisa McDermott

Serves: 2 **Prep Time:** 10 minutes **Cook Time:** 20 minutes

DAPHNE: Lisa is a lean, mean, cooking machine, and as a two-time winner of "Chew Tank," she's an old pro. After a fun-filled weekend of crafting and maybe a little drinking with the girls, Lisa likes to start the week off right with her Monday Morning Breakfast Burrito. With tons of spicy chorizo and fresh veggies, this power breakfast fills you up but won't weigh you down. Lisa even makes these delicious burritos ahead of time, wrapping them in foil and storing them in the fridge. When it's time for breakfast, she just heats them up in a skillet or toaster oven, and boom, breakfast is ready!

Cooking spray

¼ cup poblano peppers, about half a pepper

¼ cup red bell peppers, about half a pepper

½ tomato, diced

½ cup spinach

1 link fresh chorizo, cooked through, cut into bite-size pieces

Kosher salt and ground black pepper, to taste

3 eggs

1 egg white

¼ cup Mexican 3-cheese blend

1 flour tortilla (12–14 inch), warmed

3 tablespoons black beans (canned), drained and rinsed

3 tablespoons salsa (fresh or jarred)

¼ avocado, sliced (optional)

1 teaspoon chopped cilantro (optional)

1. Grill the peppers by placing on a grill or grill pan over medium high heat and cooking until blistered on the outside, about 10 minutes. Place in a bowl, covered with plastic to steam until cool enough to touch. Peel off the skin of the peppers and remove the seeds and the stems. Dice and set aside.

2. Spray a nonstick pan with cooking spray. Place over medium-low heat. Add the peppers, tomatoes, spinach, and cooked chorizo to the pan. Season with salt and pepper, to taste. Cook meat and vegetables until warmed through, and tender, about 5 minutes.

3. Add the eggs and cheese to a medium bowl. Season with salt and pepper and whisk to combine. Add the egg mixture to the pan. Cook, stirring frequently, until the eggs are cooked through and scrambled.

4. Add the egg-vegetable mixture to a warm tortilla.

5. In a small bowl, combine the black beans and salsa. Top egg mixture with the bean-salsa mixture. Add avocado and cilantro if desired. Wrap tortilla into a burrito and enjoy!

Short Rib French Toast

Courtesy of Dustin Smallheer

Serves: 4   Prep Time: 3 hours   Cook Time: 30 minutes

MARIO: OK, I'm not going to lie: when Dustin described this dish to me I thought, no way is this going to work. It breaks all of the rules. It's just not possible! Short ribs tossed with cheese and then stuffed inside bread, battered like French toast, and drizzled with maple syrup? I just couldn't wrap my head around it! And then I tasted it, and (cue the angels singing) my mind was officially blown. This is a really great dish to serve on the weekend or a special occasion because it does take a little time. But it's well worth the wait. Dustin, you are a crazy genius, my friend, and we love you for it!

1 pound short ribs

2 tablespoons light brown sugar

2 tablespoons adobo rub

2 cups beef broth

⅓ cup Manchego cheese, shredded

1 small loaf French bread

1½ cups maple syrup

6 dried chipotle peppers

1 teaspoon chipotle powder

6 eggs

¼ cup milk

2 teaspoons cinnamon

1. Blend adobo rub and brown sugar together and coat the short ribs with the mixture and let sit for 30 minutes to an hour.

2. Take short ribs and put in roasting pan. Add beef broth to pan and cook in oven at 300 °F for 1½ hours.

3. Let cool and then use your hand to pull apart the short ribs. Add Manchego cheese to shredded beef. Set aside.

4. Heat maple syrup with chipotle peppers to infuse, about 10 minutes, and set aside, keeping the peppers in. Adjust seasoning to taste with chipotle powder.

5. Take your French loaf and cut into 4 2-inch slices. Cut a slit into the bread for your short rib mixture. Take your mixture and stuff the bread until the mixture sticks out slightly over the bread.

6. Take eggs, milk, and cinnamon and make mixture for bread. Take your French toast, put in a baking dish, and pour egg mixture over the bread. Let sit for at least 1 hour so egg can soak all the way through.

7. Once bread is soaked through, cook in a large nonstick skillet over medium heat for 2 minutes on each side. Make sure to flip on each side of the bread crust as well to cook the egg through.

Crème Brûlée French Toast

Courtesy of Katie Cullen

Serves: 6–8 **Prep Time:** 10 minutes **Cook Time:** 45 minutes **Inactive Cook Time:** 12 hours

CARLA: OK now, this is one of those dishes that I'm kind of mad I didn't think up myself because it's such a good idea! Katie grew up eating this dish at home on the weekends with her family; and now that she's grown and engaged, she's keeping that tradition going with her hubby-to-be. Katie takes a classic—yet boozy—crème brûlée custard and dips in thick slices of Italian bread, then layers it in the caramelized sugar and bakes it into one perfectly rich and satisfying meal. Make it the night before and just pop it into the oven in the morning and you're good to go. Serve it with maple syrup and whipped cream; or if you're feeling really decadent, add a little vanilla ice cream.

½ cup unsalted butter

1 cup brown sugar

2 tablespoons corn syrup

1 loaf of Italian bread

8 eggs

2 cups half-and-half

1 teaspoon vanilla extract

1 teaspoon triple sec

1 teaspoon brandy

¼ teaspoon salt

Maple syrup and whipped cream (optional)

1. Melt butter in a saucepan. Mix in brown sugar and corn syrup. Stir until sugar is melted. Pour into a 9 x 13 baking dish.

2. Slice bread into equal slices and remove the crust. Place in baking pan into a single layer.

3. Whisk together the eggs, half-and-half, vanilla extract, triple sec, brandy, and salt. Pour over sliced bread. Cover and refrigerate overnight.

4. In the morning, remove the dish and bring to room temperature.

5. Preheat oven to 350 °F.

6. Bake uncovered 35–45 minutes in preheated oven until puffed and golden brown.

7. Serve with maple syrup and whipped cream.

Lemon Ricotta Pancakes

Courtesy of Ruth Sottille

Serves: 8   **Prep Time:** 10 minutes   **Cook Time:** 15 minutes

DAPHNE: This recipe screams summer to me. I love to eat pancakes, but when it's hot outside, I want something light. Don't get me wrong, these pancakes are jam-packed with flavor, but they won't weigh you down or make you want to crawl back into bed and take a nap like some heavier versions might. The ricotta makes them light and airy, and the lemon curd and fresh berries give Ruth's dish a brightness that is refreshing and just delightful. If you're skeptical of calling pancakes refreshing, well, then you'll just have to try these. One bite and you'll know exactly what I mean.

1 cup cake flour

1 tablespoon baking powder

¼ teaspoon fresh ground nutmeg

¼ teaspoon salt

4 tablespoons sugar

1 cup ricotta cheese

2 eggs

⅓ cup whole milk

1 lemon, zest and juice

1 tablespoon melted butter, for griddle

1 6-ounce jar lemon curd

2 cups mixed, fresh berries

2 tablespoons powdered sugar, for dusting

1. Combine the flour, baking powder, nutmeg, salt, and sugar in a large bowl and set aside.

2. In a medium bowl, combine the cheese, eggs, milk, lemon juice, and zest. Mix wet ingredients with dry until just combined.

3. Brush melted butter on a hot griddle and add a 3-ounce ladle full of batter to the griddle. Brown each pancake on both sides, about 3 minutes per side, and remove to a plate.

4. Cover the pancakes to keep warm while you heat the lemon curd in a microwave safe bowl in the microwave. Drizzle over pancakes and garnish with fresh berries and a dusting of powdered sugar.

TIP: Don't throw out extra pancakes; freeze them individually and when ready to eat, just pop them in the toaster or toaster oven and warm them through. You'll have the convenience of instant pancakes and the joy that comes with knowing you've made them yourself. —**Carla**

Chocolate Pancake Sandwich

Courtesy of Alana Rice

Serves: 6–8   **Prep Time:** 5 minutes   **Cook Time:** 5 minutes

MICHAEL: When I imagined Alana's recipe for chocolate pancake sandwiches, I thought, sure, two pancakes with some chocolate in the middle, no big deal. I was wrong; it's a huge deal! Alana introduced me to her sandwich grill that takes basic pancake batter to a whole new level. These beautiful little pockets are no ordinary pancakes, my friends. They are stuffed with chocolate chips and baked into these heavenly little pillows. And when you bite into them, all of the melted chocolate just oozes out. I get excited just thinking about it and all of the possible flavor combinations: chocolate-hazelnut, strawberry jam, ham and cheese. Alana, you've changed my life!

1 cup pancake mix (store-bought)

2 eggs

⅔ cup milk

1 teaspoon vanilla extract

2 cups mini chocolate chips

SPECIAL EQUIPMENT:

Sandwich grill

1. Preheat a nonstick sandwich grill to medium heat.

2. Place the pancake mix into a large bowl and add the eggs and the milk and whisk to combine.

3. Stir in the vanilla and pour some pancake batter into each of the 4 triangle-shaped spaces inside the preheated sandwich grill. Sprinkle a few chocolate chips in the middle.

4. Cover the chocolate chips with a little more batter. Close the griddle and cook until golden brown.

5. Serve and eat on the go.

Chocolate Hazelnut Ricotta Crepes

Courtesy of Mario Batali

Serves: 6–8 **Prep Time:** 20 minutes **Cook Time:** 30 minutes **Inactive Cook Time:** 20 minutes to 1 hour

MARIO: I serve this dish at some of my restaurants, and I'm often asked if these crepes are breakfast or dessert? My answer: does it matter? They're delicious, so why not eat them for breakfast, lunch, and dinner. I'd even eat them standing in front of the fridge as a late-night snack. Which is why when *The Chew* viewer Sara asked me for an easy, sweet breakfast to satisfy the whole family, this was the first dish that came to mind. It's got a rich, creamy chocolate filling that is tucked inside a light-as-a-feather crepe, perfectly balanced and unbelievably delicious. And look, if you don't have the time to make crepes from scratch, the store-bought ones are a fine alternative. I won't tell if you don't.

½ cup hazelnuts, finely ground

¼ cup all-purpose flour

1 pinch of salt

1 cup whole milk

2 eggs

4 tablespoons butter, melted, plus more for pan

FOR THE CHOCOLATE HAZELNUT RICOTTA FILLING:

2 cups ricotta, drained

1 cup chocolate hazelnut spread, plus extra to garnish

2 tablespoons powdered sugar

1 teaspoon vanilla

1 pinch of salt

½ cup toasted hazelnuts, chopped, to garnish

1. In a large bowl, whisk together the flour and ground hazelnuts and a pinch of salt.

2. In a separate bowl, whisk together the milk, eggs, and 4 tablespoons butter. Pour the liquid mixture into the flour mixture and whisk until combined and there are no lumps. Allow the batter to stand for 20 minutes to an hour.

3. Melt a pat of butter in small nonstick sauté pan over medium heat. Pour 2–3 tablespoons of batter into pan and swirl to coat.. Cook until pale golden on the bottom, about 1 minute. Flip and cook just 5 or 10 seconds on the second side. Remove and set aside on a plate.

4. Continue the process until all the batter has been used. (At this point you can freeze the crepes. Wrap stacks of up to 20 crepes tightly in plastic and then in foil; when ready to use, thaw overnight.)

FOR THE CHOCOLATE HAZELNUT RICOTTA FILLING:

5. Combine all ingredients except hazelnuts in a bowl and mix well to combine. Set aside.

6. Fill each crepe with some of the chocolate hazelnut ricotta mixture and fold in half.

7. Garnish crepes with a drizzle of chocolate hazelnut spread and some chopped hazelnuts.

Make-Ahead Mexican Strata

Courtesy of Carla Hall

Serves: 6–8   **Prep Time:** 15 minutes   **Cook Time:** 45 minutes

CARLA: I offered this make-ahead recipe to *The Chew* viewer Melissa, who came to us in desperate need of a new dish to make for weekend brunch with the ladies. Now, like most of us, Melissa is busy and doesn't have time to spend all day working in the kitchen. This *strata*, which is just a fancy word for casserole, is perfect because it's packed with big, bold flavors and can be assembled the night before and then baked in the morning right before guests arrive. It was a huge hit, and now Melissa's only problem is that the ladies want her to host the brunch every weekend.

1 tablespoon butter,
for buttering dish

4 cups corn bread (store-bought),
cubed

12 eggs

2 cups milk

½ teaspoon ground cumin

1 teaspoon fresh chopped
oregano, plus ¼ cup to garnish

1 cup cherry tomatoes, halved

1 jalapeño, seeded and
thinly sliced

1 can black beans (15 ounces),
drained and rinsed

2 cups cheddar cheese, grated

1 cup Cotija cheese, crumbled,
to garnish

2 tablespoons cilantro, chopped,
to garnish

Kosher salt and ground black
pepper, to taste

1. Preheat oven to 400 °F.

2. Butter a 9 x 13 baking dish.

3. Add the corn bread cubes to a baking sheet and place in the oven to toast for 10–12 minutes, until golden brown. Remove pan to cooling racks and allow to cool completely.

4. To a large bowl, add the eggs, milk, cumin, and oregano; then whisk to combine and season with salt and pepper. Add the tomatoes, jalapeño, black beans, toasted corn bread cubes, and cheese. Stir to combine.

5. Pour the egg mixture into the prepared baking dish. Press the corn bread cubes into the egg mixture to submerge.

6. Cover baking dish with foil. Place in the oven to bake until the eggs are set about 30 minutes. Remove foil and bake an additional 15 minutes until golden brown. Remove from oven and let cool slightly. Garnish with Cotija cheese and cilantro.

Toasted Almond Ricotta Fritters

Courtesy of Michael Symon

Serves: 6–8 **Prep Time:** 10 minutes **Cook Time:** 15 minutes

MICHAEL: I developed this dish for two *Chew* viewers who wanted to learn an easy way to make doughnuts at home. Well to be honest, real doughnuts take a long time to make and can be a little intimidating. I created these ricotta fritters that are just as delicious as a real doughnut but take a fraction of the time, and the self-rising flour eliminates the need for yeast. In fact, you may already have most of these ingredients in your fridge right now. These take about 25 minutes to make and about 30 seconds for your family to eat. So go on, get cooking!

2 quarts vegetable oil

1 cup sheep's milk ricotta

2 eggs

1½ tablespoons granulated sugar

1 pinch kosher salt

¾ cup self-rising flour

¼ cup toasted sliced almonds

¼ cup honey

2 oranges, zest and juice

1 tablespoon powdered sugar for dusting

¼ cup mint leaves, torn, to garnish

1. In a large heavy-bottomed pot or Dutch oven, preheat oil to 365 °F.

2. In a large bowl, stir together the ricotta, eggs, granulated sugar, orange zest, and salt. Gently stir in the flour and almonds until incorporated.

3. Using 2 spoons, drop heaping tablespoons of batter into oil. Fry in batches to avoid overcrowding the oil. Cook for 3–4 minutes or until deep golden brown. Transfer to a paper towel–lined plate, to drain excess oil.

4. Meanwhile, in a small saucepan, add honey and the juice of 2 oranges, and place over medium heat. Gently stir to combine until the sauce is heated through.

5. Sprinkle fritters with powdered sugar and drizzle with honey orange sauce and fresh torn mint. Serve warm.

VIEWER TIP: Hey guys, *The Chew* viewer Zakaya has a great tip for oatmeal on the go. She just makes big batches on the weekends, divides the oatmeal into muffin tins, and tops with her family's favorite toppings—and into the freezer they go. Just pop in the microwave, when you're ready to partake, and you've got yourself a healthy breakfast in just seconds. **—Clinton**

CHAPTER 2

Amazing Appetizers

Here's what I've learned about you, the viewer, after five seasons of working at *The Chew*: you are just like me, busy and your time is important to you. I totally get that. When you come home from a long day at work, the last thing you want to do is spend all night in the kitchen. Prepping for a party is no exception.

If I've said it once, I've said it a thousand times, the key to throwing a great party is a happy host. If you're not happy, your guests wont be, so do yourself a favor and take it easy. Don't decide to serve twenty appetizers and two mixed-to-order cocktails just to impress your friends. If they are really your friends, they will be happy with cheese and crackers and maybe some olives because the company is what's really important. Now in my opinion, every party should be a cocktail party because I love a variety of bites at my disposal at all times and I love to mingle and enjoy fabulous conversations with my favorite people.

So here, we have compiled some of our favorite viewer appetizers from the last five years. It was difficult to narrow it down to just a few, but within this chapter is a great mix of hot and cold appetizers, perfect for your next casual dinner or raging cocktail party. You'll find recipes for a casual afternoon of noshing or an elegant affair. Whatever party theme you decide, we've got it covered.

—Clinton Kelly

Warm Artichoke Dip

Courtesy of Leah Burke

Serves: 8   **Prep Time:** 5 minutes   **Cook Time:** 20 minutes

CLINTON: When I talk about being "fab on the fly," I'm talking about people like you, Leah! What's beyond fabulous about this dish, besides being insanely delicious, is that in just around twenty minutes, and with ingredients you can find in your pantry and freezer, you've got a hot appetizer ready to go when guests drop by. I'm all for shortcuts, and frozen artichokes are one of my favorite time-savers because they're classy; and frankly, no one will be able to tell the difference and you'll actually get to enjoy your party instead of working away all night in the kitchen. And that's what life should be, a party!

12 ounces frozen artichoke hearts, thawed and chopped

1 cup feta cheese, crumbled

¼ cup canned pimentos, drained and chopped

1 clove garlic, minced

1 cup mayonnaise

⅓ cup Parmesan cheese, grated

Kosher salt and ground black pepper, to taste

½ baguette, sliced and toasted

1. Preheat oven to 350 °F.

2. In a large bowl, combine the artichoke hearts, feta, pimentos, garlic, mayonnaise, and Parmesan cheese. Season with salt and pepper and place in a baking dish.

3. Bake for 10 minutes and then remove the baking dish from the oven and stir the dip. Continue to bake for another 10–15 minutes until golden brown and bubbling.

4. Serve with toasted baguette.

THE CHEW APPROVED

Grandma's Empanadas

Courtesy of Irene Santana-Rivera

Serves: 8   **Prep Time:** 30 minutes   **Cook Time:** 30 minutes   **Inactive Cook Time:** 30 minutes

MARIO: This is the kind of dish that I live for! I love it when people take the traditions they grew up with and add a twist that just makes it their own. Irene's grandmother used to stuff her turkey on Thanksgiving with ground meat, spices, and chickpeas, all tossed with a super-flavorful *sofrito*. But who wants to wait for Thanksgiving to eat these delicious flavors? Now that Irene has ten grandkids of her own, she's turned that stuffing recipe into little hand pies, perfect for feeding lots and lots of hungry little kids. It's also a great activity to get the whole family in the kitchen.

FOR THE *SOFRITO* SAUCE:

½ red bell pepper,
seeds and ribs removed

½ green bell pepper,
seeds and ribs removed

2 cloves garlic, peeled

½ small onion, quartered

½ bunch cilantro

4 leaves culantro (optional)

½ bunch parsley

FOR THE FILLING:

2 tablespoons olive oil

½ pound ground pork

½ pound ground veal

½ pound ground beef

½ teaspoon salt

½ teaspoon garlic powder

½ teaspoon onion powder

½ teaspoon cumin

½ teaspoon tumeric

½ teaspoon white pepper

FOR THE *SOFRITO* SAUCE:

1. Place all ingredients in a blender. Blend until a smooth paste forms. Remove and set aside. This will last in the refrigerator for up to a week.

FOR THE FILLING:

2. Coat a large sauté pan with olive oil. Over medium-high heat, brown the meat in batches, about 5–7 minutes per batch, stirring occasionally so that the meat doesn't burn.

3. Once browned, add the spices. Next, add the chicken broth and 2 tablespoons of *sofrito*, mixing well to incorporate. Add the capers, olives, wine, and chickpeas and stir in the tomato sauce. Simmer until the mixture begins looking like a dry chili, about 15 minutes. Allow to cool to room temperature.

TO ASSEMBLE:

4. Place a large spoonful of filling into the center of your empanada dough, pulling the edges up so that the sauce doesn't spill. Fold in half and secure edges with a fork. The empanadas should resemble half-moons.

5. Heat an inch of vegetable oil in a high-sided sauté pan over medium high heat. Fry each empanada about 2–3 minutes per side or until golden brown. Remove to a paper towel–lined plate. Serve warm.

½ cup low-sodium chicken broth

2 tablespoons *sofrito*

1 tablespoon capers

5 tablespoons green Spanish olives stuffed with *pimentón* (paprika), chopped

¼ cup red wine, such as merlot

8 ounces tomato sauce

1 14-ounce can chickpeas, drained and rinsed

1 pack frozen empanada dough (4-inch circles), defrosted

Vegetable oil for frying

VIEWER TIP: Busy Mom Cherisse has a great tip for organizing snacks for the kids. Just portion them out into zip-top bags and place them in a shoe organizer, and drape that over the door of your pantry. Now you've got snacks for the whole week and your kids can help themselves when they're hungry for a mom–approved after-school treat! **—Carla**

Mini Filipino Egg Rolls

Courtesy of Myrna Razak

Serves: 8   Prep Time: 15 minutes   Cook Time: 10 minutes

DAPHNE: What a perfect cocktail party dish! I always say that when you throw a cocktail party, you should always have something dippable, something chilled, and something fried. These crispy bites are just the appetizer to have on your table. They are easy to prepare, and you can roll them ahead of time and keep them in the freezer for any impromptu gathering.

1 quart canola oil, for frying

½ pound ground beef

½ pound ground pork

½ cup water chestnuts, chopped

½ cup green onions, finely chopped

1 tablespoon garlic powder

1 tablespoon onion powder

1 egg white, beaten with 2 teaspoons water

Kosher salt and ground black pepper, to taste

½ cup all-purpose flour

1 package egg roll wrappers, thawed

Duck sauce or chili sauce for serving (store-bought)

1. In a large Dutch oven or heavy-bottom pot, heat the canola oil to 350 °F.

2. In a large bowl, combine the ground beef and pork, water chestnuts, green onion, and garlic and onion powders. Season with salt and pepper and set aside.

3. Place 1–2 tablespoons of filling in the center of 1 egg roll wrapper. Brush the edges of the egg roll with the egg white wash. Fold one corner over the meat and roll, tucking in edges of wrapper to create a roll similar to a burrito. Repeat with remaining filling and wrappers.

4. Working in batches, toss in flour, then deep-fry until golden brown, about 2 minutes. Remove from oil to a paper towel–lined plate.

5. Serve with duck sauce or chili sauce.

Roasted Honey, Ginger BBQ Wings

Courtesy of Akilah Abrams

Serves: 4   **Prep Time:** 15 minutes   **Cook Time:** 55 minutes–1 hour

CLINTON: You know that I can't resist a chicken wing. They are crispy and saucy, and sometimes when I eat them it's like my mind goes somewhere else. And when I come back, there's nothing left but a pile of bones scattered on the table. I don't know what it is, but that good little voice in my head just stops talking and I totally lose control. Well at least that's how I felt when I tried Akilah's roasted honey chicken wings. They are sweet and sticky from the honey but a little bit spicy from the ginger; and the flavor is so perfectly balanced that I just can't stop eating them.

FOR THE HONEY GLAZE:

⅓ cup honey

2 tablespoons barbecue sauce (store-bought)

1 teaspoon ginger, minced

1 teaspoon ginger juice

FOR THE CHICKEN WINGS:

1 pound chicken wings

2 tablespoons coconut oil

1 teaspoon kosher salt

½ teaspoon black pepper

2 cloves garlic, minced

1. Preheat oven to 375 °F.

2. Line a baking sheet with parchment paper or a silicon mat.

3. Prepare glaze by mixing all its ingredients together in a small bowl and set aside.

4. Toss chicken with coconut oil, salt, pepper, and minced garlic, to coat. Arrange chicken on the prepared baking sheet without overlapping the pieces.

5. Roast in the preheated oven for 45 minutes.

6. Remove chicken from the oven, and split the ginger glaze in half. Brush the wings with half of the glaze mixture, reserving the remaining half to serve with the finished wings.

7. Place chicken back into the oven for 10 minutes.

8. Remove and serve with the remaining glaze.

TIP: *The Chew* viewer Jackie from New Jersey has a great tip for a fresh-smelling house before guests arrive for a cocktail party. Just simmer herbs and spices like lemon, mint, and lavender (or ginger, honey, and cinnamon) in water in your slow cooker a couple of hours before your party guests get there and your house will smell warm and welcoming. **—Clinton**

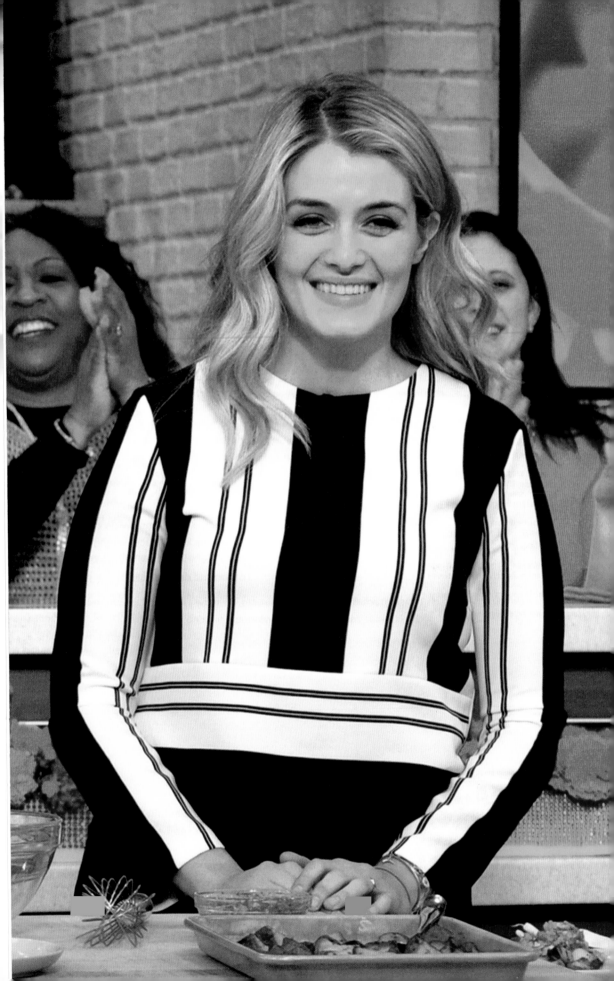

WEEK
WON

NIGHT
DERS

CHAPTER 3
Weeknight Wonders

We at *The Chew* know how hard it can be to get dinner on the table every night of the week. Some of you have picky eaters at home, or have crazy work schedules; and some of you are slightly challenged when it comes to creativity. We get it! Each of us has been there at one point or another. We know just how easy it can be to get stuck in a routine of boneless, skinless chicken breasts and frozen pizza. You know what we're talking about.

And how many times have you heard your family say, "Chicken again?" Probably too many to count.

We are here to help you! We have combed through our bank of thousands of recipes and pulled the best of the best from our viewer experts who have, by some miracle, mastered the art of the weeknight meal. These recipes are foolproof, delicious, and will have you sitting down and enjoying dinner with your family in no time. And we've even tried to choose recipes that keep the cleanup to a minimum because nobody likes to do the dishes.

Some dishes come together in less than twenty minutes, some offer a make-ahead component, and others just use some good, old-fashioned help from the grocery store. It's all about shortcuts and simplicity, quality ingredients, and some TLC. You'll be really proud of what you can accomplish with a little help from your *Chew* friends—and your family will love you for it. Enjoy!

—**Daphne Oz**

Tomato Pie

Courtesy of Kristen Baughman

Serves: 8   **Prep Time:** 5 minutes   **Cook Time:** 40 minutes

CLINTON: This is a great dish to serve during the week with a light salad. It's rich and satisfying, and it really takes no time to put together. I can also see myself eating this dish around the holidays. It would be a great addition to a Thanksgiving table. Kristen takes some classic Italian flavors, like tomatoes and basil, and folds them into a decidedly Southern-style casserole. The outcome is pure comfort.

FOR THE FILLING:

2 14-ounce cans diced tomatoes

1 small onion, chopped

1 teaspoon dried basil

1½ cups corn bread stuffing mix (store-bought)

FOR THE TOPPING:

1½ cups cheddar cheese, shredded

1 cup mayonnaise

¼ cup corn bread stuffing mix (store-bought)

¼ teaspoon dried basil

¼ cup fresh basil, chopped to garnish

1. Preheat oven to 350 °F.

2. In a large bowl, mix together the filling ingredients until smooth and transfer to a 9 x 9 casserole dish.

3. In another bowl, mix together the topping ingredients and evenly distribute over the filling.

4. Bake for 30–40 minutes, or until golden brown, and the cheese has melted. Remove from the oven and cool slightly before serving. Top with chopped basil and serve.

Fresh-from-the-Farm Coconut Carrot Stew

Courtesy of Aaron Johnson

Serves: 6   **Prep Time:** 15 minutes   **Cook Time:** 30 minutes

MICHAEL: We loved having Aaron on the show. He's a good ol' Midwestern boy (like myself), straight from the farm, and his trip to *The Chew* was his first to the big city. His stew is incredibly simple to put together, but the amount of flavor he packed into that dish is unbelievable. It's sweet from the coconut and spicy from the cayenne pepper, with curry spices that make it rich and satisfying. Make it stove top or let it simmer in the slow cooker all day long. Either way you've got a real winner on you hands.

3 tablespoons olive oil

⅓ cup white onion, chopped

3 cloves garlic, minced

1 teaspoon cayenne pepper

1½ cups carrots, cut into 1½-inch pieces

1½ cups sweet potatoes, peeled and cut into 1½-inch pieces

1½ pounds boneless chicken breasts, cut into 1½-inch pieces

1 teaspoon ginger powder

½ teaspoon curry powder

2 cans (13.5 ounces) coconut milk

1½ cups chicken stock

1 teaspoon lemon juice

Kosher salt and ground black pepper, to taste

¼ cup toasted coconut flakes, to garnish

1. Place oil in a heavy pot over medium heat. Add chicken and sauté until lightly browned, about 4–5 minutes. Add onion, garlic, cayenne pepper, carrots, and sweet potatoes. Sauté for 2–3 more minutes. Add ginger, curry powder, salt, and pepper, and stir to combine.

2. Add coconut milk and chicken stock, then bring to a boil. Reduce to a simmer and cook for 20 minutes.

3. Finish with a squeeze of fresh lemon juice and a sprinkle of toasted coconut flakes. Serve warm.

Grilled Pimento Cheese Sandwich

Courtesy of Ruth Scott

Serves: 4   **Prep Time:** 12 minutes   **Cook Time:** 6 minutes   **Inactive Cook Time:** 2 hours–overnight

MARIO: Ruth has transformed a classic Southern spread into a showstopping sandwich. She grew up in Kentucky and pimento cheese was a staple on her family's table. Now, she always tries to keep a big container of it in her fridge for a quick weeknight dinner. When you take that rowdy crowd of Southern spices and gooey cheese, stick them between two slices of buttered bread, and grill that bad boy up, something magical happens. You find yourself somewhere between fondue and *queso*, and there is no place you'd rather be.

FOR THE PIMENTO CHEESE:

½ cup mayonnaise

3 4-ounce jars diced pimento, drained

1 tablespoon dry English mustard

1½ tablespoons Worcestershire sauce

2–3 dashes hot sauce

¾ teaspoon celery seeds

¾ teaspoon apple cider vinegar

¼ teaspoon kosher salt

¼ teaspoon ground black pepper

5 cups sharp yellow cheddar cheese, freshly grated

FOR THE SANDWICHES:

8 slices white bread

8 tablespoons butter, softened

FOR THE PIMENTO CHEESE:

1. In a large mixing bowl, combine all the pimento cheese ingredients, except for the cheddar cheese, until smooth. Fold in the grated cheese and mix well. Cover and place in the refrigerator. Allow to sit for a couple of hours or overnight.

FOR THE SANDWICHES:

2. Preheat a griddle over medium-low heat.

3. Lay the bread slices out and butter each slice on one side. Spread pimento cheese onto the non-buttered side of 4 slices. Top each with the remaining 4 slices of bread. Make sure the buttered sides are facing out.

4. Place the sandwiches onto the griddle. When the bottom side is golden brown, about 2–3 minutes, flip the sandwiches. Cook until the other side is also golden brown and the cheese is heated through.

5. Remove from the griddle and cut in half on the diagonal. Serve immediately.

CHAPTER 4

Fabulous Weekend Feasts

Weekend cooking for me is all about time with the family. My boys are in their late teens now, and for the most part, they pop in and out of the house all day long. But our evenings are spent enjoying dinner together, especially on the weekends. So that's my time to get into the kitchen, early in the day, and start the process.

For me, weekend cooking is all about the low and slow dish: dishes that take a little bit longer to cook than I would have time for during the week, but that take almost no time at all to prep. Really, once you get the ingredients in the pot, the food practically cooks itself and the outcome is spectacular 99.9 percent of the time. A cheesy casserole, a pot of stew, and a big hunk of meat braised to perfection that just simmers on the stove all day long are all perfect weekend projects.

And the smells that fill the house are intoxicating; even to this day I am taken from time to time with the memories that come with a delicious meal working its magic on the stove top. You know you're doing something right when a rotating cast of family members pop into the kitchen to dip some crusty bread into your Sunday sauce or a tortilla chip or two into that pot of chili.

I'm not going to lie to you: it was difficult to narrow this category down to just a few viewer dishes. After serious debate among the hosts, we decided on some pretty heavy hitters. There are oven-baked ribs and slow-roasted pork, baked pasta dishes, and turkey with a twist. We hope that you enjoy making these dishes as much as we enjoyed eating them. *Buon appetito!*

—**Mario Batali**

SENSAT
SWE

TIONAL
ETS

CHAPTER 5

Sensational Sweets

I am incredibly impressed by our viewers' abilities to create really delicious desserts, season after season. It's funny to me because you often hear chefs say that they don't bake or that baking is not their strong point. Michael and Mario say it all the time on the show. And I think it's amazing that our viewers thrive in the world of sweets.

My favorite part about working at *The Chew* is that our discussion about food is not limited to the walls of the studio. Our viewers keep the conversation going through our social media channels and of course in their own homes. I often check the comments at the bottom of my recipes, and I see so often that people make my desserts and then discuss how they tweaked it slightly to make it their own. It really gives me an inside look at people's personalities—and to me, it feels like a conversation. I find it incredibly inspiring and it makes me feel, in some way, like I'm a part of their lives.

I've been making sweet treats for most of my life. Yet there have been so many moments where a viewer has come on the show and introduced me to an unexpected flavor combination or an old-fashioned recipe from their family that I have never heard of. I love that after so many years cooking, I am still learning.

I'm hoping that the recipes that we have chosen for this chapter will inspire you to carry on the conversation and possibly learn a little something new. And if you feel like it, add some of your own personality to these desserts, and let me know how it goes.

—Carla Hall

Strawberry Red Velvet Love Cakes

Courtesy of Sneh Kadakia

Serves: 42   **Prep Time:** 45 minutes   **Cook Time:** 10 minutes per batch

CARLA: Sneh is a really talented home baker and cooking runs in her family. Her mother was a big influence on her. She would cook all of the meals in their house. Growing up in an Indian family, Sneh learned how to cook with really bold flavors and play around with a lot of spices, especially in her sweet treats. This recipe for red velvet cupcakes is filled with delicious and warm spices that spark your palate but don't overwhelm your senses. They are decadent enough for any Valentine's Day dessert. Nothing says love better than these adorable cakes.

FOR THE CUPCAKE BATTER:

2 cups sugar

¾ cup vegetable oil

2 eggs, at room temperature

1 cup buttermilk, at room temperature

2 tablespoons vanilla extract

2½ cups all-purpose flour

1¼ teaspoons baking soda

1¼ teaspoons baking powder

1 teaspoon sea salt

1 teaspoon cinnamon

¼ teaspoon nutmeg

¼ teaspoon cardamom

2 ounces red food coloring

1 teaspoon apple cider vinegar

3 tablespoons unsweetened light cocoa powder

½ cup strawberries, finely chopped, about in ¼-inch pieces

¼ cup room temperature water (if needed)

FOR THE CREAM CHEESE FROSTING:

12-ounce cream cheese, at room temperature

4 tablespoons unsalted butter, at room temperature

2½ cups powdered sugar

½ teaspoon fine sea salt

¼ cup white pearl sprinkles, to garnish

FOR THE CHOCOLATE COVERED STRAWBERRIES:

42 strawberries (1–1½ inches long, with stems)

12 ounces dark chocolate chips

1 tablespoon cinnamon, ground

42 mini-cupcake liners

FOR THE CUPCAKE BATTER:

1. Preheat oven to 350 ° F.

2. Line mini-cupcake tins with mini-cupcake liners.

3. In a large bowl, whisk together the sugar, vegetable oil, eggs, buttermilk, and vanilla extract until combined. Next, add the flour, baking soda, baking powder, sea salt, spices, food coloring, vinegar, and cocoa powder. Add water if batter is too stiff. Whisk until smooth. Fold in the chopped strawberries.

4. Using a 2-ounce ice cream scoop, fill the cupcake tins three-quarters of the way up. Place in the oven to bake until a toothpick inserted in the center comes out clean, about 10 minutes. Remove from oven and let cool completely before decorating.

FOR THE CREAM CHEESE FROSTING:

5. In the bowl of a stand mixer, combine the cream cheese, butter, powdered sugar, and sea salt. Whisk until smooth.

FOR THE CHOCOLATE COVERED STRAWBERRIES:

6. Melt the chocolate over a double boiler. Add the cinnamon to the chocolate and stir to combine. Remove the chocolate from the heat and let stand until slightly thickened.

7. Dry the strawberries with a paper napkin to remove any moisture. Dip the tips of the strawberries into the chocolate. Place to dry on parchment paper. Don't refrigerate to prevent sweating (if using same day).

TO DECORATE THE CUPCAKES:

8. Fill frosting piper or plastic zip-top bag with frosting. Starting from the outside of the cupcake, pipe the frosting in a swirl pattern, finishing at the center of the cupcake. Sprinkle white pearls onto the frosting. Stick half of a toothpick into the side of the chocolate-covered strawberry. Stick the strawberry in the center of the cupcake and press the toothpick into the cupcake right before serving.

Pumpkin Chocolate Chip Cookies

Courtesy of Angie Shoffner

Makes: 24 Cookies   **Prep Time:** 5 minutes   **Cook Time:** 10 minutes

CLINTON: Every now and then at *The Chew* we like to put the spotlight on a viewer who really goes above and beyond for their community. Angie is totally that person. She has a really big heart and works with the East Texas Food Bank to teach nutrition classes to help families make responsible choices when accessing food. Her pumpkin chocolate chip cookies prove that dessert can be good for you, too. Packed with fiber and vitamin A, these delicious treats will help you give your kids dessert that you can feel good about.

1¾ cups pumpkin puree

1 cup brown sugar

2 eggs

½ cup vegetable oil

1¼ cups flour

1½ cups whole wheat flour

1 tablespoon baking powder

2 teaspoons cinnamon

1 teaspoon nutmeg

½ teaspoon salt

¼ teaspoon ground ginger

1 cup dark chocolate chips

1 cup walnuts

1. Preheat oven to 400 °F.

2. Mix the pumpkin puree, brown sugar, eggs, and oil until smooth. In a separate bowl, mix dry ingredients together. Add the dry ingredients to the pumpkin mixture and stir to combine. Add chocolate chips and walnuts and gently stir to combine.

3. Drop spoonfuls of the cookie dough onto a greased cookie sheet. Bake 10–12 minutes until golden brown.

Apple Crumb Cake

Courtesy of Jenny Gibbons

Serves: 24   Prep Time: 10 minutes   Cook Time: 1 hour

CARLA: Jenny makes this super satisfying apple-crumble cake every year for her family on Turkey Day. What I love most about this is that it's kind of like an apple pie mixed with a crumble baked right into a cake, so when it's dessert time, everyone's happy. And she bakes it in a big roasting pan, so it can really feed a crowd. Just assemble it in the morning, and then when your guests sit down for dinner, pop it in the oven and it will still be warm when everyone's ready for dessert.

8–10 Granny Smith apples, peeled and sliced a ¼-inch thick

FOR THE CRUST:

½ pound unsalted butter, melted and cooled

8 tablespoons sugar

2 eggs

2 teaspoons vanilla extract

2 teaspoons baking powder

3 cups flour

FOR THE CRUMBLE:

2 cups sugar

3 cups flour

2 teaspoons cinnamon

¾ pound unsalted butter, chilled and cubed

Vanilla ice cream to serve

1. Preheat oven to 350 °F.

2. Combine the crust ingredients in a food processor and pulse until dough comes together. Remove from work bowl and spread onto a 12 x 17 roasting pan, completely filling pan.

3. Shingle slice apples in 3 columns lengthwise, filling the pan completely.

4. Wipe off work bowl and blade of food processor and place back on machine. Combine the crumble ingredients into machine and pulse to form a coarse crumble. Sprinkle over apples.

5. Bake for 1 hour. Remove from oven and cool for a few minutes before serving.

6. Serve slices of cake with a scoop of vanilla ice cream.

Classic Whoopie Pies

Courtesy of Amy Bouchard

Makes: 36 Whoopie Pies   **Prep Time:** 25 minutes   **Cook Time:** 10 minutes

DAPHNE: For all of you dessert lovers out there who cut the bottom part of your cupcake off and put it on top of the icing to make a tiny little sandwich so that the frosting doesn't get all over your face (you know who you are), this is the sweet treat for you. Amy's fluffy and delicious Classic Whoopie Pies are simply to die for! In fact, her friends and family love them so much that she started her own bakery in Maine and she can barely keep these babies on the shelves. No need for a summer road trip to get a taste of this decadent dish. Amy has generously shared this recipe with all of us so we can make it for our own friends and families anytime of the year.

FOR THE WHOOPIE PIE SHELLS:

½ cup shortening

½ cup butter

2 cups sugar

2 eggs

1 teaspoon genuine vanilla or 2 teaspoons imitation vanilla

4 heaping cups sifted flour

2 teaspoons salt

2 teaspoons baking soda

1 cup sour milk or 1 tablespoon vinegar and milk to make 1 cup

1 cup cocoa

1 cup hot water

FOR THE WHOOPIE PIE FILLING:

6 tablespoons fluff

4 tablespoons vanilla

4 tablespoons flour

4 tablespoons milk

4 cups confectioners' sugar

1½ cups shortening

FOR THE WHOOPIE PIE SHELLS:

1. Mix together shortening, butter, sugar, eggs, and vanilla. Sift together dry ingredients and set aside. Add milk, cocoa, and hot water. Then mix in the dry ingredients. Scoop large rounded spoonfuls of batter onto a greased cookie sheet and space at least 2 inches apart. Bake at 350 °F for 10 minutes per batch.

FOR THE WHOOPIE PIE FILLING:

2. Add all ingredients in a bowl and beat until smooth.

TO ASSEMBLE:

3. Place scoop of filling between two of the shells and enjoy!

Berry Buckle

Courtesy of Clinton Kelly

Serves: 6–8 **Prep Time:** 15 minutes **Cook Time:** 40 minutes

CLINTON: I love a crisp, a cobbler, and a pie, but for me nothing compares to a buckle. A buckle is basically, a simple cake batter that is poured in the bottom of a pan and then sprinkled with fruit. When you put it into the oven, the cake begins to rise and the fruit starts to melt into the batter and you're left with the perfect marriage of flavors. When I was growing up, my grandmother used to make the most delicious peach buckle, and I can still remember eating it as a kid. Nothing compares to her recipe, but I'd say mine's not too shabby.

½ pound strawberries, hulled and quartered

½ pound blueberries

1 tablespoon lemon zest

4 tablespoons melted, unsalted butter, plus more for greasing pan

1 cup granulated sugar

1 large egg

1 teaspoon kosher salt

2 teaspoons vanilla extract

⅔ cup whole milk

2 cups all-purpose flour

1½ teaspoons baking powder

CRÈME FRAÎCHE WHIPPED CREAM:

1 cup heavy cream

¼ cup crème fraîche

1 tablespoon confectioners' sugar

1. Preheat oven to 375 °F.

2. Butter an 8 x 8 baking dish. Line with parchment paper that overhangs to create handles. Butter the parchment paper.

3. Place the strawberries and blueberries in a bowl and toss with lemon zest. Set aside.

4. In a medium bowl, add the melted butter and sugar. Using an electric hand mixer, beat until combined. Add the egg, kosher salt, vanilla extract, and milk. Continue to beat until combined. Add the flour and baking powder, and mix to combine.

5. Pour the batter into the prepared baking dish. Place the berry mixture on top and gently push into the batter.

6. Bake for 30–40 minutes, or until golden brown.

7. Meanwhile, prepare the crème fraîche whipped cream. In a medium bowl, combine the heavy cream, crème fraîche, and confectioners' sugar. Using an electric hand mixer or a whisk, beat cream mixture to medium peaks. Store in refrigerator until ready to serve.

8. Serve berry buckle warm with crème fraîche whipped cream.

VIEWER TIP: *Chew* viewer Maggie has a great tip for eating farm-fresh, seasonal produce all year long. Shop the farmers' markets for seasonal produce, and then when you get home, rinse them off and store them in zip-top bags in your freezer. That way you can enjoy the flavors of any season, all year long. —**Mario**

Chocolate Chip Pecan Skillet Cookie Sundae

Courtesy of Carla Hall

Serves: 6–12 **Prep Time:** 5 minutes **Cook Time:** 10 minutes

CARLA: Now where I come from, dinner isn't dinner unless there's dessert. So when I heard from *The Chew* viewer Lisa, who is tight on time but big on sweets, I knew just the recipe for her: my skillet cookies. They are kind of like a chocolate chip cookie sundae topped with chocolate, caramel, and ice cream. They're crispy on the outside and gooey in the center. And you want to know the best part? You can have them on the table in less than twenty minutes. How's that for speedy?

1 stick unsalted butter, plus 1 tablespoon, softened to room temperature

½ cup pecans

1 teaspoon salt, divided

½ cup light brown sugar

¼ cup granulated sugar

1 teaspoon vanilla extract

1 egg

1 cup all-purpose flour

¾ teaspoon baking powder

½ cup dark chocolate chips

TO SERVE:

2 pints vanilla bean ice cream

1 cup chocolate syrup (store-bought)

1 cup caramel sauce (store-bought)

Pinch flaky sea salt (optional)

1. Preheat oven to 375 °F.

2. In a medium sauté pan, add 1 tablespoon butter, pecans, and a ½ teaspoon of salt, and place over medium heat. Toast the nuts until fragrant, stirring frequently, about 2 minutes. Continue to cook until the butter has browned. Remove from heat and set aside to cool.

3. Wet Ingredients: in a large mixing bowl, add 1 stick of butter, brown sugar, and granulated sugar. Using an electric mixer, beat until well combined. Add the vanilla and the egg; stir just until incorporated. Set aside.

4. Dry Ingredients: in a separate, large mixing bowl, add the flour, baking powder, and a ½ teaspoon of salt; then whisk to combine. Set aside.

5. With the mixer on low, gradually add the dry ingredients into the wet ingredients. Using a rubber spatula, fold in the chocolate chips and the toasted pecans. Divide mixture into 6 4-inch cast iron skillets, transfer cookie dough, and spread into an even layer. Place in the oven to bake for 10–12 minutes. Remove from oven and allow to cool for a few minutes.

6. To serve, top with a scoop of vanilla ice cream, chocolate sauce, caramel sauce, and a pinch of flaky sea salt.

Summer Fruit Napoleon Trifle

Courtesy of Carla Hall

Serves: 10–12   **Prep Time:** 15 minutes   **Cook Time:** 20 minutes

CARLA: If you're looking to up your dessert game, this is the dish for you. It's visually stunning and is something that you can eat all year-round; just play around with the flavor combinations. In the winter, go with cranberries or citrus. In the spring, it can be rhubarb or strawberries. Summertime is best for using up those berries and stone fruit. And in the fall, figs or grapes are fantastic. You know what I always say when it comes to playing in the kitchen: "Let your freak flag fly!"

3 disks piecrust (store-bought), cut into 7-inch circles

1 egg, beaten

1 tablespoon granulated sugar

1 teaspoon ground cinnamon

1 teaspoon freshly ground black pepper

FOR THE SUMMER FRUIT COMPOTE:

1 cup tart red plum jam (store-bought)

1½ pounds yellow peaches, pitted, peeled, and chopped

1½ pounds plums, pitted and chopped

1½ pounds nectarines, pitted and chopped

2 lemons, zest and juice

1 teaspoon freshly ground black pepper

FOR THE WHIPPED CREAM:

3 cups heavy whipping cream

¼ cup confectioners' sugar

½ teaspoon vanilla extract

TOPPINGS:

½ cup toasted almonds

½ cup candied pecans

½ cup dried cherries

½ cup dates, pitted and quartered

½ cup dried apricots, sliced

FOR THE PIECRUST:

1. Preheat oven to 375 °F.

2. Line 3 baking sheets with parchment paper. Place piecrust on prepared sheet trays and cut in a round fitted to the trifle dish. Brush with egg wash and sprinkle with sugar, cinnamon, and pepper.

3. Bake for 15–20 minutes until golden brown. Remove from oven and place on a cooling rack to cool completely.

FOR THE SUMMER FRUIT COMPOTE:

4. In a large saucepan, add the jam and heat over medium heat. Add the peaches, plums, nectarines, lemon zest, juice, pepper, and sugar. Bring to a gentle simmer and cook until the fruit breaks down but is still slightly chunky, about 40 minutes. Remove to a bowl and allow to cool completely.

FOR THE WHIPPED CREAM:

5. In the bowl of a standing mixer fitted with a whisk attachment, place the whipping cream and whip on high speed. While the machine is running, add the confectioners' sugar; then slowly add vanilla extract and whip to soft peaks, about 4–6 minutes.

TO ASSEMBLE:

6. In a trifle dish, place 2 cups of compote, then top with 2 cups of whipped cream and a piecrust. Repeat two additional times. Garnish with whipped cream, toasted almonds, candied pecans, dried cherries, dates, and dried apricots.

Lightened Up Squash Mac and Cheese,
recite on page 82.

INDEX

Note: Italic page numbers refer
  to illustrations.